Also by Jeff Mowatt

Becoming a Service Icon
in 90 Minutes a Month

Influence with Ease
— The Total Training System

How to Manage Multiple Priorities

How to Deal with Difficult People

Influence with Ease

Jeff Mowatt, B.Comm, CSP

JC Mowatt Seminars Inc.
60 Wildwood Drive SW, Calgary, Alberta, Canada T3C 3C5
1-800-JMowatt (566-9288) www.jeffmowatt.com

Printed in Canada

ISBN 978-1-60402-645-0
National Library of Canada Cataloguing in Publication Data
Mowatt, Jeffrey C.
Influence with Ease
ISBN 978-1-60402-645-0
Business/ sales and customer service

To our little daughters

Nicole and Haley

Role models of influence

and unbridled enthusiasm

Table of Contents

Acknowledgements

In acknowledging the people who contributed to this book, I want to begin with the thousands of subscribers to my weekly *Influence with Ease®* e-mail tips. Generally, these are folks who have seen me speak, signed-up for our tips at www.jeffmowatt.com, and then provided wonderful feedback on those tips that have impacted them the most. It was their feedback that helped me choose which tips were the 'best of the best' and merited inclusion in this book.

I also want to thank those people who keep us in business—our clients of JC Mowatt Seminars Inc. I find it bizarre that organizations that most often bring me in to work with their teams are those that are already providing great service. Ironically, companies whose service stinks never bring me in. What that means is that I always learn lessons in best practices from my clients. What a wonderful relationship!

Speaking of exceptional organizations, I am forever thankful for the help and inspiration I receive from my own professional trade association, the Canadian Association of Professional Speakers. CAPS members are professionals in the highest sense. I continue to learn from this family that includes members of my home chapter in Calgary, as well as colleagues across the country and in the international federation. If you are considering bringing in a speaker for your group, your first and best source is www.canadianspeakers.org.

While on the topic of professionals, there are several experts who helped to make this book wonderfully inviting to read. Randy Glasbergen and his cartoons are witty, insightful, and I think simply the best satirical slices of business life out there. Randy can be reached at www.glasbergen.com. My talented sister, Tammy Strangemann, with her degree and experience in corporate communications, proofed and polished the initial draft. Then editor extraordinaire, Jay Winans added his brilliance for the finished product. My lifelong friend and part time photography wizard, Gerald Cole took the photo for the cover. Finally, converting this from manuscript to the book you're holding was graphic designing wonder woman Sue Krawchuck.

The person who deserves most credit for assisting with this book is my wife and business partner, Lydia Mowatt. She is the 'heart' of our family and master of knowing exactly what everyone needs. On top of managing the daily routines of our family, she also handles the administration for the company. That includes ensuring that our *Influence with Ease* tips go out to our thousands of subscribers, and managing our website so everything is kept up to date. She is amazing and I am blessed.

What's in this for you...

In your travels as a customer, you have no doubt been subjected to service providers and salespeople who have frankly left you feeling cold. They seem to be either uncaring, insincere, pushy, robotic, inept, arrogant, phony, condescending, manipulative, overbearing, obsequious, or sometimes even downright rude!

Unfortunately, it isn't always *other people* who come across negatively. Every one of us has had occasions where we would have loved to have somehow gone back in time and said something differently.

I believe the source of all these negative impressions is one thing—we have not earned the other person's trust. Without trust, it doesn't matter how good your products and services are—people won't want to pay for them. Without trust, it doesn't matter how *technically competent* you are—people won't want to listen to your advice. Without trust, it doesn't matter how *nice* you are—people won't want to do business with you.

So let's take a look at trust. Let's look at the words you choose, the actions you take that earn and hold people's trust over the long term. Of course, you already have a lifetime of experience of how to do this. I've just taken a bunch of this stuff that we all know about trust and distilled it to an approach that I call *Influence with Ease*®.

My goal for you—people may be frustrated when dealing with others, but you they trust. They're receptive to your ideas. They not only want to do more business with you but they feel more loyal to you as a person. And not just because everyone is having a good day; it happens when you're dealing with people who are tired, or rushed, and when mistakes happen and people are upset. Let's get started!

Why this stuff works...

Chances are there have been occasions in your life when your influence on others simply *flowed.* You were in conversation with a co-worker, customer, or friend, and your suggestions were readily accepted as if they were the most natural, logical solutions. It was easy.

Unfortunately, there may have been other times when you said more or less the same thing to someone else, and it went sideways. The person was inadvertently offended or unimpressed. Whatever the reason, they didn't 'buy' your product, service, or idea. Times like these, influencing others is just plain hard. That's certainly been my experience, particularly when I got my first real job.

At the age of 22 I was 'lucky' enough have been given a living laboratory for testing and studying influence. My first job, fresh out of graduating from the University of Calgary with a commerce degree in marketing, was selling one-write accounting systems for the McBee Company, door-to-door to businesses—without an appointment. Can we talk about rejection?

I remember my first week when the top salesperson of the branch, Danny Escobedo, was taking me out, showing me the ropes of cold-calling, *literally* (that week in December was punctuated with snowdrifts and a bone-chilling wind gusts). We were about to trudge into a professional building when I spotted the sign, NO SOLICITING! I pointed it out to Danny, who responded, "Jeff, if we don't sell, we don't eat. Let's get in there." You can imagine the kind of reception we received in offices where we had clearly ignored their instructions to leave them alone. In terms of rejection, let's just say I got turned down more often than a hotel bedspread!

The good news is that that job was the beginning of my training on how my choice of words and actions influenced others. I learned because I *had* to or wouldn't earn a paycheck. I also paid close attention to how others influenced me when I was a customer. I continued observing, applying, and testing these techniques over the years. And for the last 15 years as a professional speaker and customer service strategist, I've been sharing these ideas and introducing them to organizations. So, as you read these tips, just know they are not theories dreamed up by professors sheltered in academia, taught as dogma to youthful, easily impressed students. They are practices that have been tested and refined in the living laboratory of the real world. They build trust when serious money is involved and you are dealing with smart, streetwise business people who haven't the time or patience for gimmicks. This stuff has been road tested. That's why I know it works.

CHAPTER 1

First Impressions

Whether it's fair or not, people judge you on first impressions. This harsh reality is nowhere better seen than in today's ultra-fast business world where customers decide within a few seconds whether or not they trust you.

When organizations ask me to speak for their groups, I often find that there's been little or no training on how employees can enhance first impressions with customers. Managers in these companies have learned, however, that not providing this kind of training is costly. Think of the last time someone rubbed you the wrong way when you first encountered them. Chances are it took a long time for you to change your mind about that person—if ever. When people get less than positive feelings about you upon first meeting you, it curtails your career, bruises your business, and isolates your social life.

Since first impressions have such an impact, let's look at how to avoid some of the most common blunders on the telephone, with your non-verbal language, or in your word choices. You'll soon find that the first few moments are less awkward and more comfortable. Here's to great beginnings...

"You had me at HEL, lost me at LO!"

Passion that Pays

When customers like your motives, they'll want to do more business with you. In a clothing store, Haemen, the employee who was helping me, said, "I'm the manager here, I have admin stuff that I *have* to do, but what I *enjoy* doing is putting wardrobes together for customers. This is fun for me..." Result—I ended up buying three suits in one visit. Be aware that if you don't enjoy your job, your customers will know it by your body language. Everyone loses. If you want to enjoy something more, study it, and master it. *Interested* equals *interesting.*

Too Friendly for Your Own Good?

Here's a useful way to build trust when making a business call to a stranger. *"Hi, Jane, my name's so-and-so. We haven't met yet. The reason I'm calling is..."* The key is that you point out that you haven't met yet. People often receive calls from strangers who take the opposite approach; they don't introduce themselves and instead fake familiarity by asking, "How are you?" This annoys the person being called because it a) sounds insincere, and b) wastes their time.

'Politeness' that's Considered Rude

"Sir," "Miss," or "Ma'am" are terms that are often used by employees to address customers. While the employee is only trying to be polite, the customer often feels that rather being *respected,* as was intended, they feel *old.* Ideal customer relationships are more like friendships. We wouldn't call our best friend "Sir" or "Ma'am" because it creates a distance rather than a bond. In other words, when talking to customers, you can never be too polite, but you can be too formal.

"It's Casual Friday. Mind if I call you 'dude'?"

Reprinted with ©permission Randy Glasbergen www.glasbergen.com

Avoiding Sounding Scatterbrained

Here's a subtle, easy communication tip that enhances your credibility in three ways. Start the conversation by telling the person the number of points you'll make or the number of questions you'll ask. Example: "This option gives you three advantages..." Or, "There are two things I need to ask you..." Giving a specific number has three benefits: 1. Conveying that your thoughts are organized; 2. Creating anticipation in the listener; and 3. Encouraging the listener not to interrupt until you've made your points. Powerful results for a simple phrase.

There are three kinds of people:
those who can count & those who can't.

Two Words that Open Doors

One of the toughest selling challenges is converting a telephone conversation with a potential customer into a face-to-face meeting. The next time you reach that delicate point in the conversation, consider using two key words to suggest the next step. "Maybe we should *sit down* and..." The key words: "sit down." They imply that you'll be meeting in person and having a serious conversation, not a quick telephone chat. Plus, you avoid using the words "meeting" or "scheduling" since many people associate those terms with lengthy time wasters. Good results for two little words.

Get In-Sync with Customers

Managers often expect front-line employees to be friendly and upbeat with customers. While this is often a good approach, problems arise when customers are in a hurry or physically fatigued. Rushed, tired customers don't want to deal with employees who are too "chatty" or "perky." It's a turn-off. Managers would get better results by teaching employees to "mirror" the non-verbal communication style of the customer. Mirroring, when properly done, enables employees to create instant rapport, no matter what the customer's mood.

"This call may be monitored because some of our customers are really funny when they're angry."

Avoiding Wardrobe Malfunctions

The most important element in a supplier/customer relationship is trust. To help create that trust as quickly as possible, dress to suit customers' expectations. Imagine the distrust created if a plumber arrived at the customer's house dressed in an Armani suit. Similarly, a server sporting tattoos and body piercing would likely put off patrons in an upscale restaurant. By dressing to suit customer expectations you make it easier for them to be less distracted by what you're wearing and more focused on the great service you're providing. That's a win for everyone.

Do You Satisfy Their Greater Need?

Imagine shopping for household necessities with two restless preschoolers. Observing your situation, the store employee greets the children, "Hi kids, taking Dad shopping? You like colouring? How about if we set you up over here to colour while Dad finishes shopping (as she looks to you for permission)? As the parent, you'd likely be delighted. The employee generated these good feelings by focusing more on the customer's overall context (trying to be a good parent), than just dealing with the immediate concern (buying stuff for the house). When dealing with others, do you focus on overall context or merely immediate concern?

Avoiding Over-sharing

Do you or your employees ever tell customers more than they want to hear? A good indicator is the way you typically respond when customers ask, "How are you?" Often without thinking, employees reply with, "Not bad," or "60-40," or, as a security guard once told me, "I'm vertical." Yikes! When customers ask employees, "How are you?" they don't want to hear complaints. It's just a greeting. Remember that you can do yourself, your business, and the world a favour by simply choosing to be more positive when greeted by customers.

"First my ball rolled under the sofa, then my water dish was too warm, then the squeaker broke on my rubber pork chop. *I've had a horrible day and I'm totally stressed out!!!*"

Getting the Attention You Need

When phoning others for the first time, it's important to convey that you value their time and that you need their undivided attention. The challenge is that if you start the conversation with something like "Do you have a moment?" you've just given them an easy excuse to dismiss you. After all, most people are busy. Instead, after introducing yourself, ask, "You're not in a meeting are you?" The result: the other person appreciates that you're considering their time, and they have less reason to put you off. Good results for one question.

Do you 'accidentally' offend customers?

I'm bewildered by the number of managers and employees who rate their service as being *good* when it's actually borderline *offensive*. One of the most frequent gaffes involves ignoring customers. As customers, we've all been served by an employee who stops to answer the phone or talk to a co-worker. When I ask seminar participants what that behavior is called, I hear a collective response: "rude!" Employees assume this behavior is acceptable because few customers complain. That's because most customers don't complain—they just quietly go elsewhere.

Success always occurs in private and failure in full view.

Language that Customers Love

Whether it's fair or not, customers judge you by your ability to speak the local language clearly. Having a foreign accent is fine, even endearing, provided that it's not so strong that locals can't understand you. If people often ask you to repeat yourself, then you have a problem that is hindering your professional success. Do yourself and your company a favor and take language lessons until you are easily understandable. That way, customers won't have to work so hard to buy from you.

"You're a pretty good sales rep, except for the nine times you called me 'wallet' instead of 'Walter'."

Reprinted with ©permission Randy Glasbergen www.glasbergen.com

---

Winning the Hearts of the Buying Couple

Too often, employees lose business because they meet with the potential customer but not with the major buying *influencer* (often the person's spouse). One person likes your recommendation, but later the partner vetoes. The challenge is that if you suggest that the customer brings their partner, they might infer that you don't respect their authority. A way around this is to suggest that the decision is important enough that it warrants having a 'family meeting.' That saves face for the customer, shows respect for the family, and increases likelihood of a sale.

My wife says I never listen to her...
or something like that.

Share Your *Grand Intention*

Stating your "grand intention" for customers and co-workers is an easy way to add value. After adopting a dog from the SPCA, we visited a pet store for supplies. The employee began the conversation with, "I'm in this business because I love animals. So, whether you buy from here or anywhere else, I want to make sure that you get all your questions answered so that your dog gets the best possible care." Sold. Her "grand intention" made us feel that she *deserved* our business.

Husband and dog missing.
Reward for dog.

When You Need to Interrupt

Quick, who gets priority when you're talking on the phone and a visitor walks in? Answer—the visitor (who took the time to arrive in person) should receive immediate acknowledgment. That means interrupting the caller. Problem is, some folks talk so much it's hard to get their attention. The quickest way to get the caller's attention is to use a magic word—their name, "Pat, excuse me. Someone just walked in. May I put you on hold for a moment? Thanks." Then greet the visitor explaining that you're wrapping up the call. Conclude the call and take care of the visitor.

Your Phone Greeting—Fewer Words, More Impact

When you answer your phone at work do you have this habit? Do you greet the caller and then say that this is so-and-so *speaking?* If so, consider dropping the word "speaking." First, the fact that you're speaking is obvious. Second, people generally remember the words spoken last. It's more important that the caller remember your name than the fact that you're speaking. So, to have greater impact, finish your greeting by ensuring that the last word you say is your name. Example, "Customer Service department, this is Kim."

Finding Out Who's *Really* in Charge

When introducing your products or services to a new company it makes sense to start at the top. Entering an organization lower on the organization chart gets you in front of several people with the authority to say "no," but few with the authority to say "yes." In his book *Selling to the Top,* David Peoples shares a great question for determining your customer's buying authority. Next time simply ask, "Will you be making a recommendation or giving the final go ahead?" It's diplomatic and gets you more information about whom you'll need to involve in the final proposal/presentation.

"I'm not laughing at your jokes. I'm laughing at the idea that you think I have enough authority to make a decision around here!"

When Oprah Interviews You...

Here's an easy way to enhance your credibility when you're interviewed or asked a question. When you respond, first answer the question directly, *then* elaborate. Often when responding to questions, people begin by explaining all the background to their answer, and then eventually get around to answering the question. This gives the impression of skirting the issue, sometimes referred to as "sounding like a politician." Answering questions directly and then elaborating gives others the impression that you are direct, decisive, and confident.

Give me ambiguity or give me something else.

Chapter 2

The Humility Advantage

See if this applies to you or your co-workers. Your responses to requests from customers and colleagues are fast and accurate. You know your stuff: product/technical knowledge is one of your greatest strengths. If this is the case, then the bad news is that your extensive knowledge may also be one of your greatest *weaknesses*. The reason—you may be inadvertently coming across as being arrogant and insensitive.

I'm not suggesting that you have a holier-than-thou attitude. It's just that you are so quick with your answers that others feel like you haven't really been listening (even though you have). In other words, the greater your expertise, the more likely it is that you are unintentionally rubbing people the wrong way. The good news is that there's an easy way to prevent this misconception that I call *The Humility Advantage©.*

Over the years of coaching hundreds of sales and service teams, I've found there are many opportunities where a little humility pays off substantially. Try these next tips, for example, and you'll find that folks become more receptive to you and your suggestions...

"Yes, I think I have good people skills.
What kind of idiot question is that?"

How Repeat Customers Are Dangerous

Businesses often fail because service providers confuse *repeat* customers for *loyal* customers. I was a repeat customer at my local video store despite the poor service. I was unwilling to drive 15 minutes further to the competition for a simple video. The moment a competitor moved in locally, however, that first store didn't just lose some of my business, they lost it all (and that of most of their other customers). You may have repeat customers, but that doesn't mean they're loyal. If you're interested in having true customer loyalty, you can't allow your repeat business to make you complacent.

If at first you don't succeed, vigorously deny that you were even trying.

Do This *before* You Ask a Question...

A common communication blunder that turns off customers is asking them a question without FIRST explaining WHY you're asking. A hair stylist, for example, might want to know what a new client does for a living. Asking directly, however, might put off the client who thinks, "Does she want to know how much money I make?" The stylist's question comes off as impertinent. She would get better results by having the humility to first explain why she is asking. "I want to give you a hairstyle that works for your lifestyle." THEN she asks, "What you do for a living?" Now the client feels like, "Wow, she's good!"

They *Heard* You, But Did They Understand?

When giving detailed information to customers, being accurate doesn't guarantee that the message will be understood. Imagine giving lengthy route directions to a tourist who's struggling to understand the local language. Your information may be *accurate,* but there's a high margin for error in interpretation. The simplest way to ensure that someone really understands you is to invite them to paraphrase. To avoid sounding condescending, consider this approach: "I went through those directions fairly quickly. So, if you could repeat what we covered in your own words, I'll make sure I didn't skim over too much." Interesting how humility helps.

The Magic Question to Ask Your Customers

When I returned the rented car, the attendant asked, "How was the rental?" "Fine," I lied. Actually, when I initially picked up the vehicle, I waited at the counter while the staff ignored me to deal with phone customers. It wasn't worth explaining—I just figured that next time I'd rent elsewhere. Then he asked a magical question, *"What do you think we could do to improve?"* That question created several outcomes: I expressed my frustration, he apologized, reduced my bill, said they'd fix the problem, and I'll rent there again. Not bad for one question.

Reprinted with ©permission Randy Glasbergen www.glasbergen.com

I wonder if you might help me

When you were growing up, did you ever fantasize about being a hero: rescuing someone, then riding off into the sunset amidst the tearful farewells of a grateful town? That's why the following phrase works so well when you want to gain someone's cooperation. Begin with, "I wonder if you might help me?" That opening puts the other person in the position to "save the day." Most people jump at the chance to become someone's hero (especially when there's no risk for them). It's a subtle phrase that warms the hearts of even the coldest customers and co-workers.

> Friends help you move.
> Real friends help you move bodies.

The Myth of Self-Promotion

Current conventional 'wisdom' dictates that getting ahead means tooting your own horn, being assertive, and ensuring you get your due credit. It's been my experience, however, that in the real world these tactics hurt more than they help. There are no shortcuts to success. The best way to get recognition is to work hard, make a contribution, and be generous in your recognition of others. Generally speaking, people are not fools—they can see through the fluff of shameless self-promoters. Ironically, if we can resist our ego's need to get more attention, there's a good chance we may actually succeed.

> Sometimes the squeaky wheel doesn't get the grease; it just gets replaced.

Famous Last Words

If you ever watch a great leader in a meeting you may notice a subtle technique that runs contrary to common behavior. Rather than dominating the discussion on each agenda item (a temptation for ego-driven, insecure people with a title), the savvy leader merely introduces a subject, then listens for input. She observes how each member of her team contributes, debates, reasons and interacts. Then, she announces her decision, acknowledging the comments and arguments of those who've contributed. She's thereby perceived to be decisive, inclusive, and a powerful leader. When it comes to meetings, smart leaders have the last word.

"Here are the minutes from our last meeting: Marty wasted 12 minutes, Janice wasted 7 minutes, Carl wasted 27 minutes, Eileen wasted 9 minutes…"

One Word that Lightens Your Mood

Next time you're feeling harried by life's little chores, try this attitude adjustor: When listing your tasks, simply replace "have to" with "get to." "I *have to* wash my car," becomes "I *get to* wash my car." "I *have to* get groceries" becomes... (you get the idea). It doesn't take much insight to realize that you and I have it pretty good. Changing one word converts our 'burdens' into blessings. The bonus is that you can use this tool to enrich the lives of others. Compare the responses that two parents might get when talking with their child. One says, "Tomorrow, you *have to* go to school..."

Puritanism: The haunting fear that someone, somewhere may be happy.

Persuading a Know-It-All

You and I take a risk when attempting to influence someone who has a big ego. If we simply present our ideas, products, or services in the form of new information that is unfamiliar to them, there's a good chance that they will resist—not because of the idea, but because their ego may somehow feel threatened. An easy way to avoid this is to begin the conversation with, *"You are the expert on such and such. What I bring is ..."* Expressing your respect for the other person's expertise makes them more receptive to yours.

Does Your Enthusiasm Insult Their Intelligence?

"I know you've heard this a million times..." Oops! I mean, *"Perhaps you've heard this before..."* Exaggeration—otherwise known in advertising circles as 'puffery'—reduces credibility. When, in our enthusiasm, we exaggerate with statements such as *"This is the BEST..."* or *"You'll NEVER have problems with..."* or *"We ALWAYS arrive...,"* we inadvertently provoke skepticism with others. Keep in mind that using clichés that stretch the truth—even slightly (compare: *"We hear this all the time."* with *"We hear this frequently")*—we reveal our insecurities and undermine our main objective in influencing: creating trust. Tone down exaggerations. Less is more. Tell the truth. Others will reward you for respecting their intelligence.

An eternity is very, very long, especially towards the end.

Could you give me some *Advice?*

Imagine receiving this call from your financial planner. "I'm just following up to make sure that, after sleeping on it, you're still happy with the way we set up your new portfolio." After you rave about how wonderful it is, they continue, "I wonder if you could give me some advice. I'd like to offer this to other people who want sound financial planning. Is there anyone you know of..." The key to this technique is, "Could you give me some advice?" It stimulates the human need to help, and it's flattering. It's a minor phrase that creates major referrals.

"I'm looking for a mentor who can show me how to get rich without boring me with a lot of advice."

Try a Little Tenderness

As children, we all experienced the slings and arrows of being made fun of. You probably remember the humiliation of asking a question at school and having other kids make fun of you.

Those childhood scars are etched into practically everyone's psyche, including that of your customers. So next time a customer asks a 'stupid' question/objection about your products and services, take the high road. Begin your response with, "That's a great question..." You'll find that the compassion and maturity that you convey with those four simple words will be appreciated—and rewarded.

Are You *Really* a Good Listener?

Here's an easy way to gain trust with others, especially customers. As you would normally, ask the person questions to identify their needs. Then PROVE that you understand them by paraphrasing what they've said. For example, you might say to a customer, "Let's make sure I understand you. What you're looking for is..." By summarizing, you demonstrate to the customer that no one else understands them quite as well as you. That gives you an instant competitive advantage before you've even begun talking about your offerings.

Oh Lord, give me patience,
and GIVE IT TO ME NOW!

Influence Lesson from Peter Rabbit

I think my neighbor, Peter, has the right attitude about humility. He's a semi-retired family court judge who, at Easter time, would don a bunny outfit and hop into the staff's offices delivering tulips. You can imagine the staff's belly laughs echoing through the chambers at seeing Judge Peter transformed into Peter Rabbit. And they were devoted to him. As a leader trying to strengthen staff loyalty and enhance team spirit, do you use self-effacing humor? It is a risk requiring humility, security, and courage. Those are strong character traits. Maybe that's why, ironically, at an almost subconscious level we have *more respect* for those people who take themselves *less seriously*.

I took an IQ test and the results were negative.

CHAPTER 3

Selling and Persuasion

I swore to myself that I would not buy anything as I walked into the carpet factory in Delhi, India. The only reason I was entering at all was because I was part of a tour group and this was the last stop. By the time I left the factory, however, our busload of worn-out tourists had been transformed. We were energized, laughing, and most surprisingly, laden with purchases. Having sworn to myself I wouldn't buy anything, I walked out with carpet in hand having spent over six hundred dollars. The salesman in the factory had successfully created a customer feeding frenzy.

When I speak at conventions and for organizations on how to boost sales, I often talk about how customer contact employees lose potential business because of one major factor. They spend too much time trying to sell and not enough time stimulating the customer's natural urge to buy. Customers hate to be sold to but they love to buy. Like the salesperson in the Delhi carpet factory, you can spark a buying frenzy when you use these next approaches to selling and persuasion...

Caution—Needs New Muffler

Too often, salespeople believe that they should gloss over any flaws in their products and services. Ironically, pointing out the weaknesses is often a great way of building trust and generating sales. Soon after graduating from university, I attempted to sell the 'old beater' I'd been driving. My classified ad described the low-priced car as being in very good condition. Result—not one call. Upon the advice of my Dad, I changed the ad to tell the whole story, "needs new muffler." Result—numerous calls and sold the car in three days.

For Sale: Parachute. Only used once, never opened, small stain.

See if There's a Fit

A common error when beginning a sales conversation is to start talking about what the potential buyer *"might like."* The problem is that likes and dislikes are whimsical and aren't that reliable for decision making. Instead, you'll get better results when you offer to explore options with the buyer and *"... see if there's a fit."* The second phrase is easier for the buyer to agree to because it implies that you'll be systematic in helping them reach an appropriate decision.

Echo Your Understanding

Perhaps the most powerful way to influence others lies not with the way we speak, but with the way we listen. Customers will buy from people who truly understand their needs. A simple technique to help you become a better listener is the *echo technique.* After the customer makes a statement, you repeat their last few words in the form of a question. For example, a travel agent customer says, "I want to go someplace hot." Responding with, "Someplace hot?" encourages the customer to elaborate so you can make a more appropriate recommendation.

Generally speaking, you aren't learning much when your mouth is moving.

Let Me Buy You a Coffee...

If you deal with customers, consider the impact of the *reciprocity response.* Researcher Dennis Regan found that even when an employee was generally viewed as being obnoxious, if he bought his co-workers a soft-drink over lunch he was able to sell them almost twice as many raffle tickets as the employees who were likable but who hadn't given them anything prior to the sales pitch. The reason—when we give people anything for free, they are strongly compelled to reciprocate. When influencing others it's true that what goes around comes around.

The only time the world beats a path to your door is when you're in the bathroom.

Offer Less and Sell More

The conventional *wisdom* about attracting customers is to offer a wide selection. While large selection may *attract* potential buyers, unfortunately, it often *prevents* them from actually making a purchase. Columbia University researchers confirmed this when offering samples of jam. One display offered samples of six flavours of jam. In a second display they offered twenty-four. The twenty-four-sample display attracted fifty per cent more people. However, the six-jam display translated into over seven times as many sales! It seems when it comes to choice today's customers are indeed overwhelmed. Is it possible that *you* could offer less and sell more?

Three Little Words that Customers Love

One characteristic that separates amateur salespeople from professionals is that the pros *talk less* and *listen more*. A simple phrase that ensures that you do this is, *"It sounds like..."* Saying these three words forces you to paraphrase your understanding of customer needs *before* you talk about whatever it is that you have to sell. Big impact for three little words.

Help wanted: Psychic.
You know where to apply.

Thawing Customer Coolness

People often need to be warmed up before they are given new information. Otherwise, you may come across as being pushy and create resistance. Next time you're about to provide new information, begin with a "teaser" benefit. Then ask if it would be "*useful*" for them to hear about it. For example, before you describe your company's background, you might say, "It's important to know that the people you do business with are well established, so you're not left in a lurch. Would it be *useful* for you to hear about my company's background?" Now, you're not perceived to be "selling." Instead, you're providing information that's useful.

More Showing Less Telling

When influencing others, demonstrations can dramatically speed the buying process. Years ago, when I worked in the oil industry, a chemical supplier explained that he had a new form of acid inhibitor that was particularly effective. He brought lots of literature and clinical studies. But rather than get heavily into the paperwork, there in our corporate boardroom he took a sample of hydrochloric acid, mixed it with his new inhibitor, and poured it onto his bare hand. Since his flesh didn't melt off, we realized the stuff was pretty good. Sold. Ask yourself if there are ways that demonstrations could do more of your selling for you.

If at first you do succeed,
try not to look surprised.

Why Customers Like Threesomes

When selling or proposing your ideas, keep in mind the "Rule of Three." Movie theatres found that when they sold only "large" and "small" drinks, they sold equal amounts of each. To sell more of the "large" drinks, they offered a third "jumbo" size. The result—because people tend to avoid extremes they most often selected the safe middle ground, and bought "large" drinks. Translation, when you have an idea or something to sell, you'll often get better results by adding two surrounding alternatives.

Maverick Magnetism

One of the most compelling ways to sell products, services, or ideas is to challenge the conventional wisdom. When explaining a new concept to someone, point out what most people tend to believe about something, in other words, the conventional wisdom. Then show them how in reality your product, service, or idea completely invalidates the common belief. The moment you have the other person thinking, "I never looked at it that way," you've created immediate value and dramatically enhanced your credibility.

The Missing Link in Attracting Interest

Customers don't buy features, they buy benefits. "Linking phrases" help you to translate features of your product or service into benefits for your customer. Examples of linking phrases include "which means..." and "so that..." Here's how we could use a linking phrase in a sentence. "This coffee cup has a ceramic handle (feature), *which means* (linking phrase) that you won't burn your hand" (the benefit). Essentially, linking phrases are short versions of the message, "What this feature means to you..." In other words, linking phrases help you to connect more powerfully to the real needs of your customer, *which means* they'll feel more inclined to buy from you.

Cynics are people who know the price of everything and the value of nothing.

Talk about a Sale!

When offering your customers any kind of a quantity discount, you'll get better results when you choose the right wording. Example: "If you were to buy these widgets individually the price would total two *hundred and* ninety-seven *dollars*. As a package, though, you get the whole set for two forty- five." The second number sounds much lower because

a) the second and third digits are both lower than those of the initial number. And b) the package number is expressed without using the words: *"hundred," "and,"* or *"dollars."*

"If you hire me this week, I'm on special for only $3.99 a pound!"

Is Your Voice Losing Them?

One of the most awkward challenges in business is asking customers to make a decision. Often employees either avoid asking the question at all or they try a phony sounding 'closing technique.' For better results, simply ask the customer a question such as, "What do you think?" BUT ask the question as a statement. In other words, there should be no question mark in your voice. Your voice tone gives the customer a feeling of confidence and agreement. It becomes a question with a foregone conclusion.

When to Hold Your Peace

A common blunder when trying to influence others is talking too much. This is particularly true after asking a question. For example, a sales representative might "close" by asking, "What do you think?" At this point the rep needs to REMAIN SILENT. The silence may be awkward, but it's critical to wait until the other person makes that buying decision. More often than not, by remaining silent you'll receive an affirmative answer. When it comes to influencing others, silence really is golden.

Never miss a good chance to shut up.

One Word that Tweaks Interest

As you picture yourself shopping at a farmers' market, compare which of these two offers tweaks more of your interest. One vendor, while offering you a sample from a tray of jams, says, "Please try this strawberry jam." The second vendor holding a similar tray says, "Please try *my* strawberry jam." All things being the same, the jam from the second tray will taste better—not because of the flavor, but because it was served with implied ownership and professional pride. Not bad results for changing one word.

An Irresistible Proposition

When you're having a sales conversation with a potential customer, it's useful to provide three critical pieces of information. First, point out the *benefit* that your product or service provides for the customer. Second, explain what's *unique* about it. And finally, provide *evidence* that supports your claims. Together, the benefits, uniqueness, and evidence constitute what's known in sales circles as a "unique selling proposition" or USP. If you're providing information in writing, the USP should be the foundation of your proposal.

Stories that Sell

One thing a sales rep can do better than any brochure is tell personal stories about the products or services. When I went to Ridley's Cycle in Calgary to look at mountain bikes, I didn't pick the one with the most detailed spec sheet. Instead, I took the advice of the employee who was obviously an avid mountain biker. He described his experience of test riding their bikes with such enthusiasm, I ended up buying *two* (one for a friend). Brochures may be necessary, but it's *people* and *personal stories* that create instant buying behavior.

Life is nothing like the brochure.

Your Thoughts?

Ever feel awkward with customers when the time comes for you to ask for the order? Here's a great approach that an employee used with me when I was the customer. The sales rep answered my questions about various pieces of home gym equipment. I thanked her and was about to leave the store when she asked a wonderfully phrased question, "Your thoughts on the bench?" It was gentle, non-demanding, and still got the feedback she needed. Next time you need the customer's decision consider asking, "Your thoughts on...?" It's simple, subtle, and it works.

Chapter 4

Negotiating

In their book, *The Millionaire Next Door,* authors Thomas Stanley and William Danko found that ordinary people (non-celebrities) who managed to amass the most wealth were *not* those who had the highest-paying jobs. The people who became millionaires were those who managed to live significantly beneath their means. In other words, they were frugal about their spending. That doesn't mean we should be tightwads. It does, however, lend credence to the idea that it pays—literally—to learn how to negotiate.

Whether you are buying a home, asking for a raise, or discussing where you and your sweetheart should go on vacation, you are negotiating. Get it wrong, and not only can you get stung financially but you'll also harbor resentment towards the other person. Worst of all is the damage it can do to your self-image.

That does not mean your goal is to 'win' while the other person loses. That doesn't work with long-term relationships. Instead, effective negotiating means you are finding ways for both parties to have their needs met. Get ready to earn more dollars, more self-respect, *and* strengthen your partnerships with these negotiating tips...

"Lemont is our finest negotiator. Perhaps you've read his book, *The Art of Pouting*."

Reprinted with ©permission Randy Glasbergen www.glasbergen.com

---

What's Your Status?

Which of the following best describes how you, as an employee, consider your importance compared to the customer? Are you a) More important than the customer?)In this case you come across as arrogant and the customer doesn't *like* you); b) less important than the customer? (Here, the customer observes your subservient behavior and doesn't *respect* you); or c) you consider yourself and the customer to be equals treating each other with mutual respect? Option 'c' provides the only viable opportunity for friendship and respect. That's a great basis for a long-term, mutually beneficial relationship—at work or in your personal life.

Ginger Rogers did everything Fred Astaire did, only backwards and in high heels.

Let's Not Get Ahead of Ourselves

When you're selling the "invisible" —a service—avoid discussing price too soon. When a potential customer calls you and begins with, "How much would you charge for...?" you quickly become perceived as an easily replaceable commodity. Consider this response, "I'll be happy to discuss our charges with you in detail. But before we do, perhaps we should discuss whether or not my services would be a fit for you at all." Then begin asking questions to identify their needs so that you can suggest a made-to-measure solution. In other words, avoid talking price before establishing value.

Careful What You Ask For

When resolving conflict, keep in mind the old story of two sisters who each wanted the last orange. They finally split it, each receiving half. Sounds reasonable except that one wanted the peel for marmalade while the other wanted to extract the juice. Their mistake was that they concentrated on their bargaining *position*, "I want at least half." If they'd instead considered their *interests* (why they wanted it), they both would have received twice as much. The lesson: when negotiating, focus on each other's *interests* rather than *position.*

Two wrongs are just the beginning.

Gentle on the Budget Buyer

When selling a product or service, there are times when you may want to discuss the customer's budget. The challenge is that simply asking, *"What's your budget?"* may come across as inappropriate. It may sound like we're asking how much they can afford. That's like asking how much money someone earns. Or it may sound like we're just trying to find out the maximum to charge, which may not result in our receiving accurate information. A more tactful way of wording the question is to ask, *"Is there a budget that I should be aware of?"*

Disagreeing Gracefully

Imagine expressing your heartfelt, articulate opinion about an issue. The other person responds with, "Yes, *but…*" The moment we hear the word "but" most of us anticipate that not only will the person disagree with us, but that they haven't heard or valued what we just said. When negotiating, people who are perceived to be poor listeners have zero credibility. The lesson: when you disagree, replace the word *but* with *and*. So you might respond with, "Yes, *and* here's another thing to consider…" It's a way of disagreeing without being disagreeable.

"This is the nicest conversation we've had in weeks. Let's not spoil it by talking."

Is This a Proposition?

Consider this approach next time a customer asks if you can take x dollars off your price. *"I don't think there's any way I can take off x. I may be able to get y dollars off. I don't know yet. Let me ask you something. If I can manage to get it to you for y... (and again, I don't know yet—I'll have to do some checking), if I can do that for you, are we going to be moving forward with this?"* This enables you to gain commitment up front and avoid wasting time pursuing an option that wouldn't result in a sale.

When you starve with a tiger,
the tiger starves last.

Embracing Your Critics

When you disagree with a customer or co-worker, consider using the, "feel, felt, found" formula, created by Ron Willingham. The way it works is that you respond to the other person's opinion with, "I know how you *feel*. I *felt* the same way. And then what I *found* was... (then explain how you arrived at your conclusion)." "Feel, felt, found" enables you to redirect another person without harming their pride.

The Gasp Reaction

To avoid paying more than market value when negotiating, consider using the 'gasp' reaction. Let's say you're visiting a flea market and you ask a merchant how much an item costs (you assume it's eight dollars). If the merchant says, "Ten dollars," using the gasp reaction, you'd reply in a voice of astonishment, "Ten dollars!?" (That's the gasp). You then remain silent, looking at them for some sort of explanation. If they've inflated their opening price, they may immediately start lowering it, and you haven't even begun discussing what you think it's worth.

Never do card tricks for the group you play poker with.

Sewing Seeds of Collaboration

When someone asks you to reduce your price or provide a concession, make sure to request that they do the same. One approach is stating, "We want to come up with an arrangement that will work for you and for us. You do agree that both parties need to have their needs met, right?" Wait for their agreement. "So, if we do that for you, then a way you can help us is..." Key: you set the stage for win/win by asking, "You do agree that both parties need to have their needs met, right?" Simple question. Powerful results.

"Let's compromise. You do everything I say and I'll say everything you do."

Reprinted with ©permission Randy Glasbergen www.glasbergen.com

I Had in Mind

A common mistake when negotiating with others is expressing your opening offer as a firm commitment. For example, if you say that you think that a rocking chair is only worth ten dollars, then you've basically eliminated your ability to pay more without losing face. Instead, a phrase that opens more options is, *"I had in mind,* paying ten dollars." Saying that you *had it in mind* enables you to start the negotiations at a certain level, while giving yourself and the other party room to continue negotiating.

I have enough money to last me the rest of my life unless I buy something.

Offering to Walk Away

When attempting to persuade, if you find that you seem to be pursuing an option while the other party sounds lukewarm, try this approach. After again describing the potential benefits to the other party ask, *"Is this something you'd like to explore, or would you rather I just let the idea drop?"* This politely forces them to make a baby-step commitment to the process or stop wasting everyone's time. Most often, you'll find they respect your consideration as well as your willingness to walk away. Realistically, there's very little to lose and a lot to gain when you use this question to determine their level of commitment.

What about *My* Needs?

Buyers sometimes persuade sellers to reduce prices by saying, "We only have a budget of x dollars." If you decide to lower your price, it's important to receive some sort of *consideration*. Otherwise, the buyer may think that a) Your prices were too high in the first place, or b) Next time they'll automatically get the same lower price. In other words they win/you lose. So, if you do lower your price consider saying, "Sure I can do that for you, and for that I'll need..." That way you create win/win and maintain the perception of price integrity.

If I Asked You Politely

Whether you're dealing with a customer whose cigar smoke is disrupting other patrons, or a chatterbox seated behind you in a movie theatre, it's useful to have a way to resolve the problem without causing offence or creating a scene. One of the most effective techniques I've discovered is using the phrase. "I was wondering *if I asked you really politely*, if you might..." By pointing out that you're asking politely you demonstrate that you are respectfully asking a favor. That permits the offending party to comply without losing face.

I've had fun before. This isn't it.

Getting a Little Respect

When you're a customer receiving poor service, don't settle for "talking to the manager." You're likely to get better results by going straight to the top. Write a letter directly to the president of the company thoroughly explaining the circumstances. Indicate on the letter that you are copying the local manager. Then to speed the process, fax (rather than e-mail) the letter to both parties. This approach makes the local manager more accountable to quickly solve your problem and to prevent it from reoccurring.

It's been lovely, but I have to scream now.

The Power of Quiet Rage

Someone once said that 'anger' is not a four-letter word. This is particularly so when someone's oversight or foul-up has caused you unnecessary inconvenience or suffering. The key is to EXPRESS your anger—DON'T DEMONSTRATE IT. When you can quietly explain to someone, without shouting or swearing, that you are furious, you are apt to be taken seriously. By using this approach, you appear to be calm, rational, and justifiably angry. You've become a person who deserves to have their problem solved immediately.

Therapy is expensive. Poppin' bubble wrap is cheap. You choose.

Are You For or Against This?

When introducing new projects to a team, consider this approach I learned from my dad about gaining buy-in. A Saskatchewan farm boy who quit school at grade ten, Dad eventually founded and led CEDA, one of Canada's largest industrial service companies. He maintains that when you run a meeting, don't just debate, then *assume* there's consensus. That means those who argued against a decision can later undermine the project, stating they never liked the idea at the outset. Instead, go around the table asking each person to vote for or against the proposal. That way, even those who argued against a concept at the beginning are now on record as supporting it. I found as I've chaired boards, this technique is wonderfully effective at ending debate—and dissension.

Never test the depth of the water with both feet.

Chapter 5

Superior Service

If you're a service provider (and who isn't at one level or another), keep in mind a life lesson from high school. Namely, that your *interpersonal skills* largely determine how well-liked you are. Unfortunately, many people still assume they can get by strictly on their technical skills. But customers can get technical information on the Internet. When engaging services, they need to feel that the chemistry is right.

A customer's feeling of being *well-served* doesn't happen because they merely get what they want to buy. It happens when service providers pay attention to a few choice details. Let's look at several that will not only ensure you're more highly regarded at work—they'll also serve you well in social settings.

"That's our mission statement. If people follow that, everything else seems to fall into place."

A Lesson from Grandma

It's easy to forget the personal touch in today's high-tech world of e-mails, form letters, and receipts featuring happy faces that say "Thank you." That's why now, more than ever, you can have greater impact with colleagues and customers when you go the old-fashioned route. Differentiate yourself by consistently sending brief *hand-written* notes of thanks, congratulations, or it was a pleasure meeting you. Hand address the envelope and lick the stamp. Amidst all the bills, correspondence, and glossy junk mail, your note will foster the friendly feelings of getting a letter from Grandma.

Need a Hug?

Quick, according to studies at the University of Texas, what single gesture increased waiters' and waitresses' tips by an average of thirty-six per cent? Answer: they physically touched the patrons at some point during the meal. Picture touching a customer on the upper arm while asking, "How's the food?" Of course, you have to be careful about who and where you touch (a handshake is usually safe). It appears that in our techno-automated, cyber- society most people still appreciate—and are willing to pay extra for—service with a personal touch.

Reprinted with ©permission Randy Glasbergen www.glasbergen.com

Phrases to Let Go Of

Have you ever caught yourself beginning a statement with a phrase like, "The truth is...," "Honest...," "I really mean this...," "To tell you the truth," or "Believe me..."? They all essentially announce that we are about to tell the truth, implying that everything we've said up till that point has been a lie! These types of statements tend to hurt rather than help our credibility. The best way to avoid sending these mixed messages is just omit these prefaces and say what's on your mind.

Look Deeply into My Eyes

Here's an easy way for employees to be remembered when thanking customers. Avoid the amateur routine of giving the customer their change, receipt, or bag, and saying, "Thank you" as they leave. Instead, consider the approach used by a clerk when I was the customer. Before handing me my change, she held on to it until I looked her in the eye. While maintaining eye contact she smiled, nodded, and said, "Thank you." *Then* she handed me the change. Result—she appeared more sincere. And her store seemed more deserving of my patronage than the average business.

You Look Marvelous!

Ever given someone a compliment that backfired? That's where you say something nice to someone and they interpret it to be insincere flattery. This often happens because the compliment was *general* in nature, for example, "You look nice today." To avoid this, rather than offering *general* compliments (or criticisms, for that matter), you'll get better results when you're *specific,* for example, "That handbag looks great—it matches your outfit and shoes perfectly." Being more specific has the effect of making you appear to be less a flatterer, and more a perceptive, considerate individual.

"You're more beautiful today than you were the day I met you. You had a really big pimple that day."

Rest Easy, My Liege

Whenever one person gives someone else a task to do, there's always the risk that the other person might "go through the motions" to get it done. Whether you're an employee doing something for a customer or for your supervisor, your choice of words can instill confidence or foster mistrust. For example, if you respond to a request with, "I'll do it," it sounds like you're forced to do something. Instead, use the phrase, "I'll *take care* of it." That response implies that you're complying because *you care,* and that you'll see it through until completion.

The only substitute for good manners is fast reflexes.

My Pleasure

To improve the impression you make upon customers, coworkers, or anyone else, use these two words more often. When someone thanks you for something, rather than responding with the standard, *"you're welcome," "yup,"* or worse, *"uh-huh,"* look the person in the eye, smile, and say, *"My pleasure."* Saying *"my pleasure"* takes no more time or energy than the other responses, yet it makes you sound like you are much more positive and willing to help.

Stop Checking Your BlackBerry!

In today's world of BlackBerrys, cell phones, and people's ears being hardwired into iPods, the skill of listening is rarer and more highly valued than ever. With so many people 'multi-tasking' (not being fully attentive to the person they are talking with), customers are craving to be fully listened to. You aren't really listening when your phone is vibrating or if you take a call while a customer is waiting. You aren't really listening if you're just waiting for your turn to talk. Real listening means not just hearing the words, but attempting to sense the emotion behind the words. When you've fully listened to someone, you'll speak with more than *understanding*; you'll speak with *compassion*. When it comes to influence, talk is cheap. It's listening that's rare and valuable.

Multitasking: screwing up several things at once.

You Did That for Me?

Quick, name two words that, when frequently used by waiters and waitresses, increase tips by twelve per cent. Answer: "for you." Rather than saying, "Would you like some more coffee?", the savvy server says, "I brought more coffee over *for you.*" The patron perceives the service to be more personal and tips accordingly—on average twelve per cent more. That's what I call easy money. And it's a great way of increasing your perceived value with customers and co-workers without working harder.

Who's *Really* Paying Your Wages?

Most airlines understand the value of treating their best customers extra special. They provide faster check-ins, access to executive lounges, and first-class seating. Other businesses don't seem to understand the principle. Grocery stores, for example, routinely make their best customers stand in line the longest, while providing "express" service to people with small purchases. Other businesses ignore the customer who arrives in person and instead pick up the phone to take care of the customer who just phones in. Ask yourself if your daily business practices consistently nurture your best clients or (unwittingly) neglect them.

I have seen the truth,
and it makes no sense.

Take Ten Before & Ten After

Here's a tip I learned while speaking for the Canadian Franchise Association from Rolly Morris, president and CEO of Krispy Kreme Doughnuts Canada. Their policy is that they are open for business and answering phones ten minutes before the posted opening. And they remain open and answering phones ten minutes after posted closing. They call it "10 Before/10 after". That way, you don't disappoint customers who arrive three minutes early (no arguing about whose watch is right). And customers don't feel rushed out the door—or barred from entering—as closing time approaches. It's a simple way to generate good feelings—and extra revenue.

"I have to come in late this morning, but I'll make up for it by leaving early this afternoon."

The Misnomer of Customer 'Loyalty' Programs

Here's a statistic about customer buying behaviors that may surprise you. *The Financial Post* cited the findings of the Acumen Research Group on the value of customer "loyalty programs." Loyalty programs are frequent shopper programs that give awards and discounts based on customers' total purchases. The study found that loyalty programs were the second to last reason (twenty-one out of twenty-two) why customers return. Value and good service got the highest marks. In other words, 'loyalty' programs aren't. They create some *repeat* customers, not necessarily *loyal* customers. True customer loyalty is largely based on the way businesses deliver the intangibles.

Why do doctors call it practice?

"Anything Else I Can Do for You?"

Here's a wonderful phrase that separates service professionals from people who are just going through the motions. In this case the employee was coordinating the conference room at a hotel where I was speaking. When he and I had finished going over the audio/visual set-up, he cheerfully offered, *"Anything else I can do for you?"* By using that phrase, he demonstrated that he wasn't just an employee who needed to set up a meeting room; he was a professional sincerely interested taking care of a customer. Simple sentence. Big difference.

I'll Be Happy To!

What would you say if a customer asked for an item and you didn't know if it was available? The common response of an untrained employees is, "I don't know, I'll *have to* check." The professional, however, responds with, "I don't know, but I'll be *happy to* check." If you were the customer, which employee would you say provides better service? The lesson: simply changing your language from "have to" to "happy to" is another way of enhancing your perceived value—without working harder.

The Soft Sounds of Spending

We all know that when it comes to increasing our revenues, we need to pay more attention to the details. Turns out those details may be easier and more profitable than we assumed. *The Journal of Consumer Research* reports that restaurants that played *slower* music increased the average overall bill by a whopping twenty-nine per cent! Is your business paying enough attention to the details of your customers' senses? In today's fast-paced world, soft background music may make your business an oasis where customers want to slow down and spend more.

Honk if you love peace and quiet.

Chapter 6

When Things Go Wrong

As you reach this last chapter, you may be thinking, "These tips sound good when dealing with *normal* people, Jeff, but you don't know the kind of angry/upset customers I have to deal with!"

For the record, I do understand what it's like to deal with upset customers. Years ago, I owned a line of vending machines that would occasionally break down, and when customers phoned to complain, some would start by swearing at me. Worse, while attending university, I worked part-time as a bouncer at a nightclub and the odd *over-served* customer who didn't like club rules would even take a swing at me. So, I do have some experience with angry customers.

If you are a business owner or manager, I implore you to invest some real training in this area. Unfortunately, when it comes to dealing with dissatisfied customers, most business owners and managers believe that money-back guarantees and/or exchange policies will fix the problem. Lousy strategy. Money-back guarantees and exchanges may fix the problem, but they do nothing to fix the relationship. Policies don't fix relationships—people do.

I'm gob-smacked at how few managers realize that they need to train employees on why and how to fix the damaged relationship when we let a customer down. The consequences of this are staggering. Inadequately trained employees chase away repeat customers and referrals, spread damaging word-of-mouth advertising, and become frustrated and de-motivated because they're constantly dealing with upset customers. Front-line turnover skyrockets. What a mess!

On the other hand, we've found that when we equip our clients' teams with just a few critical people skills, front-line employees create such *positive* feelings for both themselves and their customers that upset customers become even more loyal. They are transformed from being a *critic* of your organization to becoming an *advocate*. Everyone wins. So for this last chapter, let's look at how to reduce everyone's frustration and increase customer loyalty when things go wrong…

"Please leave a message and I'll call you back as soon as I can tolerate the sound of a human voice again."

Reprinted with ©permission Randy Glasbergen www.glasbergen.com

I Messed up—Badly

While serving as president of the Canadian Association of Professional Speakers, I received a remarkable 'bad news' call from one of our event organizers: "Jeff, I wanted to talk to you about a situation that has just come to my attention. I want you to know that I accept full responsibility for the foul-up. It was a stupid mistake that I shouldn't have made and I will do everything that needs to be done to fix the error. What happened was . . ." Since he was already berating himself, my response could only be magnanimous. Accepting full responsibility, while recognizing the consequences of the error, shows that you're prepared to "take your lumps" like a grown-up. People respect that.

Customer *Concern* Department

No one likes to hear customers *complain*. Employees become impatient and defensive when faced with these "trouble-makers." One of my seminar participants equated listening to customer complaints to undergoing amateur eyeball surgery. (That can't be good.) To prevent this defensive mindset, employees need to be trained to treat customer complaints as *concerns*. Employees need to know that customers who express concerns are helping you to stay sharp and competitive. Focusing on customer *concerns* versus *complaints* will immediately shift a potentially negative situation into one that is positive and productive.

Worry is a misuse of the imagination.

If You Hear a Complaint, You Own it

Compare three employees who receive complaints from customers about the building's sidewalk being icy. Biff: "I know! It's a good thing *I* didn't slip!" Bill: "Sorry, I'll contact the janitor." Buffy: "Sorry, I'll take care of it right away." She then contacts maintenance. When maintenance finishes, they inform

Buffy. She then phones the customer, "Just wanted to let you know that we cleared up the ice. Thanks again for informing us—you may have prevented an injury." Result: Buffy turns an unhappy customer into a fan simply by taking ownership.

If things get any worse, I'll have to ask you to stop helping me.

"The trouble with this company is nobody wants to accept responsibility for anything. But don't tell anyone I said that!"

Fair Isn't Equal

When training and consulting for various organizations, I find, unfortunately, that many employees adopt the attitude that everyone should be treated fairly and equally. If you share that opinion, consider this. Imagine the disastrous consequences if parents gave their six-year-old child the same liberties as their sixteen-year-old teenager. "Make sure you're home from grade one by midnight." Yikes! Parents understand the concept that we should treat all our children fairly, but certainly not equally. I think we'd do well to adopt the same perspective at work with employees and customers. Fairness is essential, but equality is overrated.

The rooster crows, but the hen delivers the goods.

Let's Start over Again

Consider this approach when dealing with a disappointed customer. Your mission is not just to fix the customer's problem or to keep their business; it's to mend the relationship. Imagine the reaction of the customer when you slowly and sincerely state, "We don't want to just regain your business, we want to regain your trust. So, what would it take for you to trust us again—you tell me." This approach gives the customer the control they probably felt they've lost. Plus, since it espouses the virtue of trust, it's less likely that they'll attempt to take unreasonable advantage.

The Question Better Left Unasked

When dealing with upset customers, blunders often occur when employees gather details. One of the employee's main roles is to show serious concern and to facilitate the customer's 'venting' of their frustration. That means asking the customer who, what, where, and when the problem occurred. Too often, unfortunately, employees ask customers 'why?" Usually, the answer to a *why* question is that someone was incompetent. That part of the event is better left unsaid. So, by all means ask the *four* "w"s, but avoid asking, 'why?'

> Experience is something you don't get until just after you need it.

Lighten the Load for Upset Customers

Imagine you're dealing with a company that's performing its services slower than promised. When their front-line employee attempts to fix things, which of these phrases would you as the customer find to be the most reassuring to hear: A) "I'll tell my manager about it," B) "I'll look into it," or C) "Your problem just became my problem. And I'm going to pursue this until it's resolved and you tell me that you're satisfied." No contest. 'C' conveys the take charge, responsible attitude that customers need and want to hear. Powerful results for a few words.

"Who picked 'I Can't Get No Satisfaction' to be our on-hold music?"

Reprinted with ©permission Randy Glasbergen www.glasbergen.com

What Will Work Best for You?

There are times when dealing with dissatisfied customers that you may not be able to repair the damage or inconvenience that they were subjected to. A common error when attempting to salvage the relationship is to ask, "What would you like us to do?" That phrase sounds too much as though you won't do anything unless the customer gets you to do it. Instead use the phrase, "What will work best for you?" That wording sounds much more like you're willing to do whatever it takes to make it right.

Visit our restaurant! The food's great and you'll like the ambulance

---

We Can't Overlook...

What would you tell the customer in this situation? You are a driving examiner and you have to fail an applicant because they ran a stop sign. An amateur would explain that, "*It's policy* not to pass anyone who runs a stop sign." A professional, however, would rephrase the statement to, "Running a stop sign is a safety issue that we just *can't overlook*. So, you didn't qualify today." The phrase "we can't overlook" something gives the same information as "it's policy," but sounds more reasoned and acceptable.

Before you criticize someone, you should walk a mile in their shoes. That way, when you criticize them, you're a mile away and you have their shoes.

Tone Down the Bad News

No one likes giving customers bad news. When you're the bearer of bad news, consider toning it down. Literally. Lower your voice tone and rate of speaking. Generally when people get excited or emotional about ideas, they tend to raise their voice pitch and pace. When you're giving bad news you want to give the impression that you are thinking clearly, logically, and reasonably, not emotionally, and certainly not irrationally. By slowing down the rate you're speaking and lowering the pitch slightly, you come across as the calm, quiet voice of reason.

I couldn't repair your brakes,
so I made your horn louder.

Three Words that Annoy Customers

On one of my speaking trips, an airline gate agent managed to frustrate a departure room full of passengers—using three words. He announced a short flight delay adding, "Please *bear with us.*" The phrase 'bear with us' implies that the customer is at best going to have to endure the service—not enjoy it. Worse, it sounds like giving the customer an order. Result—groans. When problems happen, better to express appreciation than give orders. The agent would have received a warmer reaction by explaining the short delay, replacing 'bear with us' with 'thank you for your patience.'

This would be really funny—
if it wasn't happening to me.

Softening Hard Feelings

Someone once said that life would be easy—if it wasn't for other people! When customers are upset, there is a simple, powerful tool that makes life easier for everyone—empathy. When customers are upset, they are often angry for two reasons: 1) They didn't get what they expected; 2) They are frustrated because they're forced to complain. So, along with solving the problem we need to acknowledge the person's frustration. Saying to a customer, "How frustrating!" or "That must have been annoying!" goes a long way to softening the hard feelings that the incident created.

"Please continue to hold. Your call will be answered in the order in which it was received, unless we hear a lot of loud, obnoxious sighing."

Reprinted with ©permission Randy Glasbergen www.glasbergen.com

Do You Confront or *Attack*?

Perhaps one of the toughest challenges in relationships is giving 'corrective feedback' to people you care about. As a supervisor, husband, and father, I've made my share of mistakes when confronting others, less so since discovering this tip: Focus your feedback on *behavior*, not attitude. Instead of saying, *"You need to be friendlier to customers."* (Friendliness is an attitude), focus on *behavior* with, *"Within five seconds of the customer's arrival, you are expected to smile, show teeth, and greet them."* Avoiding confrontation doesn't help anyone. Focus on observable behavior. As for 'correcting' the other person's attitude, what they think, believe, and feel, forever hold your peace.

Do You Want the Good News...?

One of life's more difficult tasks is giving people bad news. A common error is to start with the bad news, and then try to make it better by giving the good news afterwards. The problem is that as soon the receiver hears the bad news they become emotionally stressed. So they aren't really listening anymore when you explain the good news. Instead, when giving both good and bad news, begin with good news (so they actually hear it), then explain the bad.

I Feel Your Pain

When you have to give a customer bad news, consider revealing your own similar circumstances. A claims adjuster attending one of my seminars explained that she used to have a hard time telling some clients when their car had been stolen and damaged that they still had to pay the deductible, even though they weren't to blame. Ironically, she's had much better impact since the same thing happened to her aunt. Now, she shares her personal experience with clients, and they feel less like they've been singled out and victimized by the decision. Sometimes it's true that misery loves company.

Laugh, and the world laughs with you. Cry, and the world looks sheepish and suddenly remembers it had other plans.

I See Your Point

A service provider passed on to me a simple phrase that she uses to diffuse angry customers. After the customer expresses their concerns (vents), she confirms the details with the customer, empathizes with their frustration, and then wraps it all together with the phrase, "I see your point." Whether or not we agree with the other person, the phrase "I see your point" communicates that we've listened and that we understand their perspective. That's a big step towards preserving that valuable customer relationship. Bonus: it's also a great approach to use with family and friends.

When Breaking Unspoken Promises

It's human nature to want to avoid conflict with customers. Unfortunately, that means that too often we keep our spoken promises but ignore our assumed promises. I recall growing frustrated waiting for a prescription. When the pharmacist finally took care of me, he apologized for the long delay and explained that his assistant had just quit, so he was short-staffed. He realized that I had *assumed* that the service would be faster, and treated it as if he'd broken a promise. Result—he kept my business. If you're serious about reducing customer defections, don't ignore conflict. Make sure to address it when your business breaks *unspoken* promises.

Depression is merely anger without enthusiasm.

How to Disarm a Bank Robber

As a customer service strategist and twenty-year black belt martial artist, I love this strategy. FBI special agent Larry Carr developed the "Safecatch" system of being overly friendly to disarm bank robbers. The premise is being effusively kind to would-be robbers throws them off so much, they rethink the crime and leave. First Mutual Bank, whose employees were trained on the approach, reduced bank robberies by a whopping forty-five per cent! If kindness and compassion can literally disarm a bank robber, imagine what it does for frustrated customers.

Caution: I have an attitude and I know how to use it.

The Power of Positive Phrasing

When giving information or instructions to customers or co-workers, take a lesson from lifeguards—focus on the positive. If, while at a swimming pool, a youngster starts running on the deck, the savvy lifeguard won't say, "Stop running!" Instead, she'll say, "Walk please!" When dealing with customers, rather than saying, "We won't be able to deliver until the weekend," instead say, "We can have it for you as early as this weekend." Same information, but it's likely to be better received when offered as a positive.

Transforming Dissatisfied Customers

When a product or service fails, it isn't enough to merely provide a refund or exchange. After all, in addition to the money the customer originally spent, returning the item has also forced them to spend more time, transportation costs, and hassle. That means employees need to express empathy about the customer's frustration, sincerely apologize, and then offer something (in addition to the exchange or refund) to compensate the customer for their inconvenience. That way, you turn an upset customer into an advocate.

"Try our product for 30 days. If you're not completely satisfied, then just be grateful that you live in a country where people are still allowed to be dissatisfied!"

Last Word on Influence from Jeff

As I speak to audiences across North America and beyond about customer service, there is one overriding message that I want professionals to take away. Customer loyalty is not about being *friendly* per se; it is about creating trust. Often it's just a matter of knowing the right way to say what needs to be said. That's the easy part—which is why I call this approach and the tips in this book, *Influence with Ease®*. The harder part of building trust is not so much what you say, but what you do.

At the end of the day people trust you when they know they can count on you, no matter what.

You and I both know individuals, and even entire organizations, that seem to put more energy into making excuses than getting results. It always seems to be someone else's fault that they weren't able to deliver on their commitments. Sadly, some people live their entire lives with this world view. Hopefully they come to realize that the person they hurt the most with this perspective is themselves. They damage their own reputation.

Bob Murphy, a professional speaking colleague who passed away years ago, observed that your reputation is like a shadow. It precedes you and determines how others who have heard of you will welcome you. And it follows you wherever you go.

My hope for you is that this serves as a reminder. Make promises sparingly, and keep them *no matter what it costs you.* Don't do so out of a sense of obligation to your company, your co-worker, or even to your customer. Keep your word out of your sense of self-respect. The bonus is, you'll have a reputation for integrity and performance. That is not always easy. But it does make you trust*worthy.*

Want your team members to really use this?

You've probably heard that the best way to learn something is to teach it to others. If you are a manager or supervisor, here's an easy way to use this book to make that happen for your entire team...

When you and your team members meet, include what I call a "Coaching Moment," where someone you've selected shares one of these Influence with Ease tips with the group. After reading the thirty-second tip to the group, the person then explains:

1. Why they liked the tip,
2. How they've been applying it,
3. What the results have been.

As he or she finishes, the person then quickly picks another member of the team who will do the Coaching Moment for the next meeting.

There's nothing like knowing you'll need to *stand and deliver* in front of your peers at the next meeting to motivate an employee. It's a simple, do-able task that involves people, creates learning accountability, and focuses everyone on the big picture—strengthening customer loyalty.

By the way, if, as a manager or supervisor, you're looking for more ways to enhance your organization's sales and/or service culture, you'll find a step-by-step process (including Coaching Moments) in my management book *Becoming a Service Icon in 90 Minutes a Month* available at www.jeffmowatt.com.

Good luck!
Jeff

P.S. I'd love to hear from you with your success stories, comments, or questions. Feel free to phone me or drop me an e-mail at jeff@jeffmowatt.com or 1-800-JMowatt (566-9288).

Influence with Ease books for your team

Order additional Influence with Ease books for your team, colleagues, or as conference gifts

Standard:	1-9 books	@ $27
Wholesale:	10 books or more	@ $12

(U.S. and international orders payable in U.S. funds)

Please send us (quantity) ________ books @ ________ = ________

Shipping & Handling

$10 total for 1-5 books
$20 total 6-9 books
10-49 books @ $1.50/book
50-99 books @ $1/book
100 books or more @ $.50/book

Shipping & handling = ________

Subtotal = ________

Canadian orders add 6% GST = ________

Total Amount of order = ________

Toll free Canada and USA 1-800-JMowatt (566-9288)
local in Calgary, Canada: 403-244-9094

Fax: 403-244-9094

JC Mowatt Seminars Inc.
60 Wildwood Drive SW,
Calgary, Alberta, Canada T3C 3C5

info@jeffmowatt.com

www.jeffmowatt.com

Jeff Mowatt
In Person!
Invite Jeff Mowatt to bring his *Influence with Ease* seminar to your business or association.
Contact:
Jeff Mowatt, BComm, CSP
Toll free Canada and USA
1-800-JMowatt (566-9288)
local in Calgary, Canada:
403-244-9094
www.jeffmowatt.com

Here's what others are saying about the **Influence with Ease** presentation:

"Jeff's Influence with Ease® subject matter was a strong draw—a record turnout in our 95 year history. Moreover, of the six sessions in our full day conference, Jeff's was the most highly rated—by far!"

Melissa Secord, Manager, Communications & Special Events, Ontario Association of Optometrists

"Jeff Mowatt's session was excellent and was rated by delegates as the best of the entire conference."

Louise Shulko, Alberta Support Staff Conference Chair

"This investment in your people will pay for itself over and over."

Elaine Brownlee, Business Training Mgr, Business Development Bank of Canada

"Jeff Mowatt's name came up over and over on our conference evaluations where we asked, "Which guest speaker do you think added the most to the conference?"

Mike Dempster, Director General, Supply and Services, Gov't of Canada

"Jeff's content, delivery, high standard of professionalism, and pleasing personality makes him one of the most outstanding and memorable speakers I've heard."

Stan Palmer, Past International Director, International Assoc. of Lions Clubs